Scrumpti
Cupcakes
And
Frostings

By: Sara Winlet

See My Other Books

Breakfast Casseroles

Scrumptious Scones

Scrumptious Cookies

Scrumptious Muffins

Scrumptious Pies

Scrumptious Cookie Bars

Cupcakes have become quite popular over the last few years. Most cities have at least a few if not several cupcake stores which sell tasty but very expensive treats. This book offers a wide variety of scrumptious cupcake and frosting recipes which taste better, are easy to bake, and cost much less than those available from retail cupcake stores. With any of my cupcake recipes and minimal time and effort, you can easily bake delicious cupcakes that your family will love.

Tips:

Always fill muffin liners about 2/3 full with batter to keep from spilling over in the oven.

I like to use aluminum liners rather than paper liners as it reduces sticking.

If you don't have a pastry bag to pipe the frosting on top, cut a small corner of a zip lock bag, fill with frosting then pipe over cupcakes.

If you only have salted butter on hand, just omit the salt in the recipe.

I recommend using an ice cream scooper to fill cupcake cups with batter, to assure that every cupcake turns out the same size.

I like to make cupcakes with ingredients I already have on hand. That way you can control the ingredients.

Table of Contents

Cupcakes

Frosted Pineapple Cupcakes

You will feel like you are in the islands when you taste these Pineapple cupcakes with citrus frosting.

Ingredients:

1 1/3 cups all-purpose flour
1/3 cup shredded coconut
1 teaspoon baking powder
1/8 teaspoon salt
1/2 cup unsalted butter, softened
1/2 cup granulated sugar
1 teaspoon lemon zest
2 large eggs
3 tablespoons plain yogurt or sour cream
2 tablespoons pineapple juice
3/4 cup crushed pineapple, drained
Citrus Buttercream Frosting (see frosting section)

Directions:

Preheat oven to 325 degrees F.

In a large mixing bowl, cream butter, sugar, and lemon zest until light and fluffy. Add eggs one at a time until well incorporated. In a medium bowl, combine flour, coconut, baking powder, and salt. Add to butter mixture a little at a time, alternating with yogurt and pineapple juice. Mix well. Fold in crushed pineapple. Spoon batter into muffin liners until each is 2/3 full. Bake for 25 to 30 minutes or until set in the center. Allow to cool completely before frosting.

Coconut Mango Cupcakes

These Coconut Mango Cupcakes are so delicious. The coconut milk makes them so moist and the Mango frosting makes them extra special.

Ingredients:

3/4 cup all-purpose flour
1/2 cup shredded coconut
1/2 cup unsalted butter
1 teaspoon baking powder
1/8 teaspoon salt
1/2 cup granulated sugar
2 teaspoon lime zest
2 eggs
1/4 cup coconut milk
1/2 tablespoon fresh lime juice
1/2 cup fresh or canned mango, chopped
Mango Buttercream Frosting (see frosting section)

Directions:

Preheat oven to 325 degrees F.

In a medium bowl, cream butter, sugar, and lime zest until light and fluffy. Add eggs one at a time. Mix well. In a large bowl, combine flour, coconut, baking powder and salt. Add flour mixture into butter mixture alternating with the coconut milk and lime juice. Fold in chopped mango by hand. Spoon batter into muffin liners until each is 2/3 full. Bake about 25 to 30 minutes or until golden brown and set in the center. Cool completely before frosting.

Chocolate Pumpkin

Cupcakes

Pumpkin is not just for thanksgiving, after tasting these delicious cupcakes you will discover that you will want to eat all year long. The combination of the chocolate and pumpkin blend so well together.

Ingredients:

2 cups all-purpose flour
3 tablespoons unsweetened cocoa
1 1/4 cups packed brown sugar
2/3 cup melted butter
3 eggs
1 15oz can pumpkin
3 teaspoons baking powder
1 teaspoon baking soda
1/2 teaspoon salt
3 teaspoons cinnamon
1/4 teaspoon ground ginger
1/4 teaspoon ground allspice
1/4 teaspoon ground nutmeg
1/8 teaspoon ground cloves
2/3 cup granulated sugar

2 teaspoons vanilla extract
1/3 cup sour cream
1/2 cup semi-sweet chocolate chips
Chocolate Ganache Frosting (see frosting section)

Directions:

In a medium bowl, combine flour, cocoa, baking soda, baking powder, salt, cinnamon, ginger, allspice, nutmeg, cloves then set aside. In a large mixing bowl, cream butter, brown sugar and granulated sugar. Beat until light and fluffy. Add eggs, pumpkin and vanilla and beat for about 1 minute. Add sour cream, scrape down sides of bowl then add flour mixture and mix lightly until just combined. Fold in chocolate chips. Spoon batter into muffin liners until each is 2/3 full. Bake for 18 to 20 minutes or until set in the middle and toothpick comes out clean. Cool before dipping into ganache.

Blueberry Sour Cream Cupcakes

Fresh blueberries is what makes these cupcakes so delicious. This is one of my favorite summer time cupcakes. I like to frost them with cream cheese frosting then add a blueberry on top.

Ingredients:

3/4 cup all-purpose flour
3/4 cup cake flour
1/2 teaspoon baking powder
1/4 teaspoon salt
1/2 cup unsalted butter, softened
1cup granulated sugar
2 eggs
1 teaspoon vanilla extract
1 cup milk
1 cup fresh blueberries
Cream Cheese Frosting (see frosting section)

Directions:

Preheat oven to 350 degrees F.

In a large bowl, mix both flours, baking powder, and salt

then set aside. In a medium mixing bowl, cream butter and sugar until light and fluffy. Add eggs one at a time mixing well after each one, then add vanilla. Alternate flour and milk into butter mixture until well-blended. Fold in blueberries by hand. Spoon batter into muffin liners until each is 2/3 full. Bake for 20 to 25 minutes or until center is set and lightly golden brown. Cool completely before frosting.

Oatmeal Raisin Cupcakes

These cupcakes are great as a stand-alone cupcake, but when you put cinnamon buttercream frosting on them it really makes them even more delicious.

Ingredients:

1 cup old fashioned rolled oats
1 1/4 cups all-purpose flour
1/3 cup oat bran
1/4 teaspoon baking soda
3/4 teaspoon baking powder
1/2 teaspoon salt
2 teaspoons ground cinnamon
3/4 cups unsalted butter (softened)
1/2 cup granulated sugar
1/2 cup packed light brown sugar
2 eggs
1 teaspoon vanilla extract
1/2 cup sour cream
3/4 cup raisins
1/2 cup sweetened flaked coconut
Cinnamon Buttercream Frosting (see frosting section)

Directions:

Preheat oven to 375 degrees F.

In a medium bowl, combine oats, flour, oat bran, baking soda, baking powder, salt and cinnamon. Mix well. Then set aside. In a large mixing bowl, cream butter, brown sugar and granulated sugar until light and fluffy. Add eggs one at a time mixing well after each one. Blend in vanilla. Add flour mixture until just combined. Beat in sour cream, then fold in raisins. Spoon batter into muffin liners until each is 2/3 full. Bake for 18 to 20 minutes or until center is set and tops are golden brown. Cool completely then frost with Cinnamon Buttercream Frosting.

Traditional Red Velvet Cupcakes

My son and I love Red Velvet Cake with Cream Cheese Frosting. So, I could not make a Cupcake Cookbook without adding these delicious treats.

Directions:

1 1/4 cups cake flour
1 tablespoon cocoa powder
1/2 teaspoon salt
3/4 cup granulated sugar
3/4 cup melted butter
1 egg
1/4 teaspoon red gel food coloring
1/2 teaspoon vanilla extract
1/2 cup buttermilk
3/4 teaspoon baking soda
1 teaspoon white vinegar
Cream Cheese Frosting (see frosting section)

Directions:

Preheat oven to 350 degrees F.

In a medium bowl, combine flour, cocoa, and salt and then set aside. In a large mixing bowl, cream butter and sugar until light and fluffy. Add egg and mix well. Scrape down sides. Add vanilla and food color. Mix well. First reduce speed to low, then add flour mixture alternating with buttermilk. In a small bowl, combine baking soda and vinegar which will be foamy. Add to batter, and mix well. Spoon batter into muffin liners until each is 2/3 full. Bake for 18 to 20 minutes or until center is set. Cool completely before frosting.

Strawberry Patch Cupcakes

Strawberry cupcakes are one of my all time favorites. For the frosting I add Fresh, chopped strawberries to the cream cheese frosting. Tip: pat the strawberries with a paper towel to get off excess juice before adding into frosting.

Ingredients:

1 cup all-purpose flour
1/4 cup cake flour
1/2 teaspoon baking powder
1/2 teaspoon salt
1/2 cup unsalted butter (softened)
1 cup granulated sugar
1 teaspoon vanilla
1 egg, plus 1 egg white
1/2 cup milk
1 cup finely chopped strawberries
Cream Cheese Frosting (see frosting section)

Directions:

Preheat oven to 350 degrees F.

In a medium bowl, combine flour, cake flour, baking powder and salt then set aside. In a large mixing bowl, cream butter, sugar and vanilla until light and creamy. Add eggs, scraping sides after each one. Reduce speed to low. Add flour mixture alternating with milk. Mix well. Fold in strawberries by hand. Spoon batter into muffin liners until each is 2/3 full. Bake for about 20 to 25 minutes or until center is set and tops are lightly golden brown. Cool completely before frosting.

Fresh Peach Cupcakes

There is nothing like bitting into a fresh peach in the summer time. Thats why I love these Fresh Peach cupcakes, frost with cinnamon buttercream frosting to make them extra special.

Ingredients:

1 1/2 cups cake flour
3/4 teaspoon baking powder
3/4 tcaspoon baking soda
1/2 teaspoon salt
1/8 teaspoon nutmeg
6 tablespoons unsalted butter
1/2 cup granulated sugar
1/2 cup packed brown sugar
1 large egg
1/2 teaspoon vanilla extract
3/4 cup sour cream
2 medium fresh peach (diced)
Cinnamon Buttercream Frosting (see frosting section)

Directions:

Preheat oven to 350 degrees F.

In a medium bowl, combine flour, baking powder, baking soda, salt and nutmeg then set aside. In a large bowl, cream butter and sugar until light and fluffy. Add egg. Mix well. Mix in vanilla, scraping down sides of bowl. Add flour mixture alternating with sour cream. Mix well. Fold in diced peaches by hand. Spoon batter into muffin liners until each is 2/3 full. Bake for about 18 to 20 minutes or until center is set and tops are lightly golden brown. Cool completely before frosting.

Chocolate Orange Cupcakes

If you haven't tried orange and chocolate together than you are in for a treat. The combination is very good together. The Orange Buttercream Frosting makes them even more Delicious.

Ingredients:

1 stick of butter (softened)
1/2 cup granulated sugar
2 teaspoon orange zest
2 small eggs
1/2 cup all-purpose flour
1/4 cup orange juice
3 oz melted dark chocolate
2 oz melted milk chocolate
Orange Cream Cheese Frosting (see frosting section)

Directions:

Preheat oven to 350 degrees F.

In a large mixing bowl, cream butter, sugar, and orange zest until light and fluffy. Beat in eggs one at a time scraping sides of bowl after each one. Add flour, orange juice and melted chocolate mix for about 2 minutes. Spoon batter into muffin liners until each is 2/3 full. Bake for 15 to 20 minutes or until set in the center. Cool completely before frosting.

Harvest Pumpkin Cupcakes

These cupcakes are not just for Fall, I love to eat pumpkin goodies all year. The pumpkin puree makes these cupcakes moist and decadent. Frost with Cinnamon Cream Cheese Frosting to make them extra delicious.

Ingredients:

2 cups all-purpose flour
1 cup granulated sugar
1/2 cup packed dark brown sugar
2 teaspoons baking powder
1/2 teaspoon salt
1 teaspoon Cinnamon
1/2 teaspoon ground nutmeg
4 eggs
1/2 cup milk
3/4 cup caned pumpkin (plain)
1 stick unsalted butter (softened)
Cinnamon Cream Cheese Frosting (see frosting section)

Directions:

Preheat oven to 350 degrees F.

In a medium bowl, combine flour, sugars, baking powder, salt, cinnamon and nutmeg then set aside. In a large mixing bowl, cream butter, pumpkin, eggs and milk until well blended. Add flour mixture. Mix well. Spoon batter into muffin liners until each is 2/3 full. Bake for about 20 minutes or until center is set. Cool completely before frosting.

Luscious Lemon Cupcakes

These Lemon Cupcakes, topped with a delicious Citrus Buttercream Frosting is a sweet tart combination that you will love.

Ingredients:

3 cups all-purpose flour
1 teaspoon baking powder
1/2 teaspoon salt
2 sticks of unsalted butter (softened)
2 cups granulated sugar
4 large eggs
3 tablespoons lemon zest
2 tablespoons lemon juice
1 teaspoon vanilla extract
1 cup buttermilk
Citrus Buttercream Frosting (see frosting section)

Directions:

Preheat oven to 350 degrees F.

In a medium mixing bowl, cream butter and sugar for about 1 minute. Add eggs one at a time mixing well after each. Beat in vanilla and lemon zest. In a medium bowl combine flour, baking powder and salt. Add flour mixture to butter mixture alternating with buttermilk and lemon juice. Mix well. Spoon batter into muffin liners until each is 2/3 full. Bake for about 20 to 25 minutes or until center is set and tops are golden brown. Cool completely before frosting.

German Chocolate Cupcakes

German chocolate cake with Coconut Pecan Frosting is an all time favorite. The combination of coconut and pecans makes them so delicious.

Ingredients:

2 cups cake flour
1 teaspoon baking soda
1 1/2 sticks unsalted butter
1/2 teaspoon salt
4 medium eggs
1 1/3 cups granulated sugar
1 1/2 teaspoon vanilla extract
1 cup buttermilk
5 oz semi-sweet chocolate chips(melted)
German Coconut Pecan Frosting (see frosting section)

Directions:

Preheat oven to 350 degrees F.

In a medium mixing bowl, cream butter and sugar until light and fluffy. Add eggs one at a time mixing well after each one. Beat in vanilla, scrape sides of bowl. In medium bowl, combine flour, baking soda and salt. Add to butter mixture alternating with buttermilk. Mix well. Beat in melted chocolate until well combined. Spoon batter into muffin liners until each is 2/3 full. Bake for about 18 to20 minutes or until center is set. Cool completely before frosting.

Chocolate Chip Cupcakes

Chocolate Chip cupcakes are always a favorite. I like to frost with Chocolate Buttermilk Frosting.

Ingredients:

2 cups all-purpose flour
2 cups packed brown sugar
1/2 cup butter
1 cup milk
1 teaspoon salt
1 teaspoon baking soda
1 teaspoon vanilla extract
2 eggs
2 cups semi-sweet chocolate chips
Chocolate Buttermilk Frosting (see frosting section)

Directions:

Preheat oven to 350 degrees F.

In a medium mixing bowl, cream butter, sugar, eggs and vanilla until light and fluffy. In a medium bowl, combine flour, salt and baking soda. Alternate flour mixture and milk into butter mixture. Mix well. Fold in chocolate chips.

Spoon batter into muffin liners until each is 2/3 full. Bake for 15 to 20 minutes or until center is set and tops are golden brown. Cool completely before frosting.

Chocolate Cupcakes With Peanut

Butter Fudge Frosting

As you know chocolate and peanut butter is a great combination. With these chocolate cupcakes with the Peanut Butter Fudge Frosting, will soon become one of your families favorite.

Ingredients:

1/4 cup unsalted butter (softened)
2 cups granulated sugar
2 eggs
2 cups all-purpose flour
3/4 cups cocoa
1 teaspoon baking powder
1/4 teaspoon salt
1 cup milk
1 teaspoon vanilla extract
2 teaspoons baking soda
1 cup boiling water
Peanut Butter Fudge Frosting (see frosting section)

Directions:

Preheat oven to 350 degrees F.

In a medium bowl, combine flour, baking powder, and salt. Mix well. Then set aside. In a large mixing bowl, cream butter, sugar and eggs until light and fluffy. Add cocoa scraping sides well after mixed. Add flour mixture into butter mixture alternating with milk and vanilla. In a small bowl, combine baking soda and boiling water. Add to batter. Batter will be thin. Spoon batter into muffin liners until each is 2/3 full. Bake for about 18 to 20 minutes or until center is set. Let cool completely before frosting.

Zesty Orange Cupcakes

These cupcakes taste like a little bit of summer, I enjoy them with the Orange Buttercream Frosting. But, they would be great with Cream Cheese Frosting also.

Ingredients:

1 1/2 cups all-purpose flour
1 1/2 teaspoons baking powder
1/4 teaspoon salt
1/2 cup unsalted butter (softened)
2/3 cup granulated sugar
3 eggs
1 1/2 teaspoon vanilla extract
1/2 teaspoon orange extract
2 tablespoons orange zest
1/2 cup milk
Orange Buttercream Frosting (see frosting section)

Directions:

Preheat oven to 350 degrees F.

In a large mixing bowl, cream butter, add sugar and orange zest, beat until light and fluffy. Beat in eggs one at a time scraping bowl after each one. Add vanilla and orange extract. Mix well. In a medium bowl, combine flour, baking powder and salt. Add flour mixture to butter mixture alternating with milk. Mix well. Spoon batter into muffin liners until each is 2/3 full. Bake for 18 to 20 minutes until center is set and tops are lightly golden brown. Allow to cool completely before frosting.

Pecan Pie Cupcakes

These cupcakes taste just like pecan pie. With very few ingredients they are quick, easy and very delicious. You can serve them by themselves or frost with Cinnamon Cream Cheese Frosting.

Ingredients:

1 cup packed brown sugar
2/3 cup butter (melted)
2 eggs
1/2 cup all-purpose flour
1 cup chopped pecans
Cinnamon Cream Cheese Frosting (see frosting section)

Ingredients:

Preheat oven to 350 degrees F.

In a large mixing bowl, cream butter, sugar and eggs until light and fluffy. Add flour. Mix well. Fold in pecans. Spoon batter into muffin liners until each is 2/3 full. Bake for 18 to 20 minutes or until center is set and tops are golden brown. Allow to cool completely before frosting.

Frostings

Chocolate Ganache

Ingredients:

1/2 cup whipping cream
1 tablespoon butter
1 tablespoon granulated sugar
1 cup semi-sweet chocolate chips

Directions:

In a medium sauce pan, combine whipping cream, butter and sugar, bring to a boil. While stirring constantly to make sure sugar dissolves. Remove from heat. Place semi-sweet chocolate into a bowl. Pour warm cream mixture over chocolate and let stand for 5 minutes. Stir until smooth. Let cool before using.

Cream Cheese Frosting

Ingredients:

1/2 cup unsalted butter, softened
6 oz cream cheese, softened
2 cups powdered sugar
1/2 teaspoon vanilla extract

Directions:

In a medium bowl, cream butter and cream cheese until fluffy. Add vanilla. Mix well. Add powdered sugar until well incorporated and achieves a spreading consistency.

Cinnamon Cream Cheese Frosting

Add 2 tablespoons Ground Cinnamon to
the above recipe.

Cinnamon Buttercream Frosting

Ingredients:

1/2 cup butter (softened)
1 teaspoon vanilla
2 1/2 cups powdered sugar
1 to 2 tablespoons milk
2 teaspoons ground cinnamon (to taste)

Directions:

In a medium bowl, cream butter until light and fluffy. Add vanilla and cinnamon. Beat in half of powdered sugar and 1 tablespoon of milk. Mix well. Beat in the remaining powder sugar, using the remaining milk to achieve a frosting consistency.

Citrus Buttercream Frosting

Ingredients:

2 tablespoons butter, softened
1/4 cup cream cheese
the zest of 1 lemon
1 cup powdered sugar
1 teaspoon lemon juice

Directions:

In a medium mixing bowl, cream butter, cream cheese and lemon zest until light and fluffy. Add powdered sugar. Mix well. Add lemon juice and mix to achieve spreading consistency.

Mango Buttercream

Frosting

Ingredients:

1/2 cup butter, softened
1/8 cup milk
1/2 teaspoon vanilla
3 cups powdered sugar
1/2 cup mashed mango
1 tablespoon lime juice

Directions:

In a medium bowl, cream butter until fluffy. Add vanilla, mango and lime juice. Mix well. Gradually add powdered sugar alternating with milk until mix achieves a spreadable consistency.

Mascarpone Frosting

Ingredients:

16 oz mascarpone cheese
1 1/4 cups heavy cream
1/2 cup powdered sugar

Directions:

In a medium bowl, cream mascarpone cheese, cream and sugar for about 5 minutes or until mix achieve a spreadable consistency.

Orange Buttercream

Frosting

Ingredients:

8 oz cream cheese (softened)
1 cup powdered sugar
1 tablespoon orange juice
1 tablespoon heavy cream
zest of one orange

Directions:

In a medium mixing bowl, cream together cream cheese, powdered sugar and orange juice until well combined. Add heavy cream and orange zest. Beat until mix achieves a spreadable consistency.

German Coconut Pecan Frosting

Ingredients:

1 can sweetened condensed milk
3 egg yolks
1/2 cup butter
1 teaspoon vanilla
1 cup sweetened coconut
1 cup pecans (finely chopped)

Directions:

In a medium sauce pan, combine milk, egg yolks and butter over low heat until thickened. Stir constantly. Remove from heat, add vanilla, coconut and pecans. Mix well. Cool completely before using.

Chocolate Buttermilk Frosting

Ingredients:

1/4 cup butter
3 tablespoons buttermilk
3 tablespoons cocoa
2 1/4 cups powdered sugar
1/2 teaspoon vanilla extract

Directions:

In a medium sauce pan, combine butter, cocoa and buttermilk. Bring mixture to a boil. Stir constantly. Remove from heat. Whisk in powdered sugar and vanilla until smooth.

Peanut Butter Fudge

Frosting

Ingredients:

3 cups powdered sugar
3/4 cup cocoa
1/8 teaspoon salt
6 tablespoons milk
2 teaspoons vanilla extract
1/3 cup butter (softened)
2 tablespoons smooth peanut butter

Directions:

In a medium bowl, cream butter, sugar, cocoa and salt. Add milk, vanilla, and peanut butter. Blend until mix achieves a spreadable consistency.

John 3:16 For God so loved the world, that he gave his only begotten Son, that whosoever believeth in him should not perish, but have everlasting life.

Printed in Great Britain
by Amazon.co.uk, Ltd.,
Marston Gate.